BROKEN SCABS

BROKEN SCABS

Book #1 of the "SCABS" poetry series

poetry by
L.Q. Murphy

illustrated by
Stacy Hummel

L.Q. MURPHY ♦ CALIFORNIA

BROKEN SCABS
Copyright © 2022 by L.Q. Murphy. All rights reserved.
Published by L.Q. Murphy

All rights reserved. No part of this book may be reproduced or used in any manner without express written permission from the copyright holders. Except for use of quotations in a book review.

This is a work of fiction. This book is sold with the understanding that the author and/or illustrator is not providing advice or demonstrations to the reading audience. Always seek professional consultation.

DEDICATION

This book dedicates the poetic words to the remarkable people who dare to recover from the battlefield scars of life.

Table of Contents

BROKEN SCABS .... *I*

DEDICATION V

Acknowledgments XIII

Introduction XV

"Human Tendencies" 1

Hi. 2

I had lived 3

Just relax bro 4

Intimidating tree. 5

The park is so joyful 6

Interesting why 7

The wise 8

Yes. 9

Fall down 10

When a cat be high 11

Breathing in. 12

Slice and dice. 13

Awake in the morning 14

Doctor 15

Drowning down. 16

The flame 17

Some men. 18

Everything goes 19

I'm ~~tired~~ 20

One and two 21
I need the honey 22
Sniff around my bush 23
Oh... her 24
But it's night, right? 25
Here is the light. 26
Too much time has passed 27
"Like Pulling Scabs" 28
Drowning my scabs 29
Each hour 30
Buzzy-buzz 31
In my cross hairs. 32
Where do we go? 33
.... 34
Something subsides inside of me 34
A silly destiny for a man 35
~~Left hand~~ blown away 36
Till my past 37
No shadow. 38
I wrote it down 39
I cut my eyelids 40
Pushing my cart. 41
Will I sleep this night? 42
My house. 43
Flying 44
Blood puddles 45

Growing hills 46

Head kicking towers 47

"The Nature of the World Stage" 48

~~Too real~~ to be a scheme 49

I panned for gold 50

The soul of my shoes 51

As I travel this deep valley of streams 52

Welded 53

~~Soggy limp limb~~ 54

Brittle twig 55

No starch 56

~~Stepping through~~ my garden 57

Bright is the flowers 58

I lost myself 59

The earth was flat 60

Making a world 61

We are leaves 62

When the heat comes 63

I'm the shade 64

Lightning spears 65

Thoughts are streams 66

Pump that gas 67

The dirt piles 68

Funny bunny 69

Sunny days 70

~~Raindrops~~ touch my skin 71

IX

A soaked letter 72

Nasty rain 73

Distant clouds thunder 74

Everything starts with dirt 75

From rain 76

My breathing release 77

The sun ~~*and the hills*~~ 78

Grandma knew I'd write her today 79

Chasing a bunny 80

If 81

It is orange you say 82

The whys of life 83

How many lives has the ocean consumed? 84

No Better Than "Who" 85

Today is day 86

~~*Not the*~~ *strongest swimmer* 87

Doing time 88

I'm back to this red brick home 89

Vroom-vroom 90

I hide from fright 91

Running about the flurry hill 92

Within the same day 93

Read this 94

Jingle. Keys jingle. 95

My tail 96

There are two 97

X

The tree branches...98

Pitter-patter 99

~~What~~ is it you ~~ask~~? 100

"Abstract Exposer" 101

Do I owe you my soul? 102

More questions ~~than me~~? 103

The wind that pushes 104

My soul knows better 105

Watching my pearls 106

Was I told 107

I told my little garden friends 108

Ax in my right hand 109

Many dreams ~~sewn~~ 110

Born and born 111

Too old 112

I think I'll die at night 113

I ~~don't~~ want to sleep 114

My eyesight ~~vacates~~ 115

The sharp everlasting pain 116

Speed limit 117

Touch down 118

Intense cases 119

One...120

Rub the furry bunny 121

I will get there 122

On the fast side 123

XI

In your face *124*

The end? *125*

The END. *126*

Author *127*

written by, L.Q. Murphy *128*

Afterword *130*

Acknowledgments

There are too many to thank, but I would like to thank my friends and family first if I began someplace. They have sacrificed so I can be myself every day.

The people I respect are the ones that found a way to climb to the top echelons of society. Here is a list of people who did not let their dire environments hold them to a lower standard of living: Denzel Washington, Oprah Winfrey, Robert L. Johnson, Nipsey Hustle, Malcolm X, J.K. Rowling, Colin Powell, Mike Tyson, Steve Harvey, Floyd Mayweather Jr., Judge Joe Brown, Robert T. Kiyosaki, and Napoleon Hill. They left clues to follow for success. Clues that help to improve their living conditions.

This is what I can relate to. I can respect the people who want to help every person who desires to improve their life. Real-world heroes consider the lives from the lowest classism to the lives in the highest stratosphere of classism. These are the people I tend to acknowledge the most.

And I cannot forget to thank the universe and that highest power in the universe that continues to let me live and breathe another day. Thank you.

Introduction

This book is built from five areas of life. Each chapter is a unique collage of thematic illustrations told with words and art.

The poetic verses in each chapter bring to life the gifts of life's experiences.

Human Tendencies draws attention to those things only humans seem to do. Our human ways. Each poem is a story told from a different perspective attempting to help you relate.

Like Peeling Scabs is about the raw pain of life, those moments we have all felt of peeling a youthful scab from your skin. Painful and nasty. It's bloody. The piercing portion of life.

The Nature of The World Stage exposes the raw brutality of worldly life forms and Mother Nature.

No Better Than Who is about our human nature to compare ourselves to each other. We fight amongst each other, yet never get to the root of the issue. In this section you will be introduced to imagery that is at the root of the comparison issue.

Abstract Exposer spotlights the fragments of human nature that are sometimes so misunderstood. This section can only be communicated using fascinating, uncompressible poetic stories. Although challenging to comprehend the message at first, the reader will have acquired the most elusive prize of life at the end... communication with the deepest part of the soul.

Within each chapter many themes are covered such as failure, love, contempt, jealousy, envy, admiration, regret, joy, and ability.

Yes, there are many more themes that might be interpreted. Don't be afraid to form your own opinion and conclude your own lesson. Beauty is in the eye of the beholder.

XV

This is the beauty of life. You are free.

I hope to travel this road of life with you. I hope my presentations appease you.

Like the poems within, it's time to comprehend the sum.

"Human Tendencies"

Are you human? Yes? Then these poems are meant to represent the things that humans tend to do, say, and/or feel.

Hi.

Hello there.
I need
Extra time.

Where did time go?

My time far from sublime.

I've been sick
My heart yearns.
I've had scabs
And deep burns.

I've had cuts
To my arteries.

I've had cuts
That'll break armories.

HUMAN TENDENCIES

I had lived
A day ago
Tomorrow ways
The ways I know

A broken heart

        Leaving the past
        My shopping cart
        Full of scabs

                In a world
              ~~Where my pain~~
                  ~~Just refuses~~

                                    ~~To be last~~

Just **relax** bro
A seamstress builds
A daiquiri bro

We'll paint
The Vegas night.
We'll finally
Do it right

With clean clothes
And **pampers.**

You know how
To do it
Right?

In**timid**ating tree.
Sealed in white bark.
At least forty feet tall.
Your "**Bark**" was stark.

A kid.
You caught me there.
I did not know.
I thought wood forever.

I thought **forever** appear.

I had a way to say and say
My "MacGyver" pocket knife
Carved my initials

The letter "L"
The letter "M."

And for years
The youthful memories remained
But your bark got old
And the memories
They went cold.

The re**pair** of your bark
Was my sad loss
And just like that
A forever memory
Was lost.

BROKEN SCABS

The park is so joyful
My friends I keep with me
But when friends are disloyal
Life turns to a frenzy

HUMAN TENDENCIES

Interesting why
Smoke comes **this** way.
Distorting the eye.
D**i**storting my way.

Tripped up and **scar**red.
This moment that frays.
To wish **for** those
Everlasting **days**.

Even with**in**
This **sight**less realm
My compass **calls**
And controls the helm.

Dislodging **these scabs**.
Chopping **smoke away**.
My blood still dripping
As I find my way.

The wise
The brain
The visual

&

The rain

I stand before
The crashing waves.

        Chest held higher than the clouds
        With rage deeper than caves.

            Does home bring hope?
            Or do I stay with the shore?

                My castle only made of sand

                But still, I'll fight this war.

Yes,
I do.

Yes,
~~I drink daily.~~

                        I ~~have tried to~~ stay away

                            ~~But when~~ I do

                                I turn to clay.

So, I stay ~~hydrated~~

Everyday...

That's my day.

Fall down
Fall up
Spin and touch

    Jump down
    Jump up
    Cheer **and** fuss

        Run down
        Run up
        Blow **and** Huff

            Climb down
            Climb up
            Grunt **and** puff

When time gets ruff

We have to **move**
Rapid stepping
With or without shoes.

When a cat be high

Does the dog go by?
When a kitty cat cries
Does a **human** walk by?

The pets that roam
Around our **home**
They keep our heart
And tell a poem.

But the love that seeps
    An **owner** keeps
A game of kindness

We play for keeps

Breathing **in**.
Deep down.
Hit **the** head.
Hit the **crown**.

Slice and dice.
He said.
She said.

That right.
Ok.
I guess.

Find the piece.
The piece... Dude?
What piece?

The last half of the fallopian tube.
Clip and cap, right?
Right. Right?

Slice and dice
He said.
She said.

The **world** changing capability.
Look around.
And around.

Slice and dice.
Right?
Wait.

Not right!
They both yelled.
They both yelled.

Awake in the morning

Up comes the sun

Lay down in the evening

Dreams are the sum

Doctor
More technical
Than I.

It's over.
I'm intuitive.
I perceive.
Please don't lie.

I can see.
Eyes see.

They **see**.
My fee.
My turn.
It's me.

Do me a favor.
Let **them** know
I tried.
I did my best.
I'm **going**.
I'll be back.

Off the **shore**
In to the sea.
I'll be lost.
But, guess what?
I'll find my way.
You'll see.

You'll see.

Drowning down.

That gurgling sound.

                              Drowning down.

                                    That gurgling **sound.**

The flame
Of my heart
Dances
With a shark.

Some men.
Oh my,
Some men.

With **moods**
so crude.

Thieves
Of hearts.
Pawning **souls**
In the land
Called rude.

Some men.
Oh my,
Some men.

It seeps deep
This mud.

Puddles red.
The blood.
A **killer's** flood.

Some men,
Oh my,
Some **men**.

It seeps deep.
A lake of tears.
Baptize the soul.
Amen!

HUMAN TENDENCIES

Everything goes

    Everyone knows

        Everything goes

            Trust ~~me~~

              Everyone ~~knows~~

BROKEN SCABS

I'm ~~tired~~
~~Of~~ being humble
Each time I ~~do~~
I tumble

        Up that way
        I fumble

        My logic is fried
        I mumble

Eye sight down
I tumble down

It hurts so bad
I fall
And crumble down

        But when I crumble down
        I always tumble down

All the way down

        Back to humble

Back to the ground

One and two.

That's three for you.

One mouth.
Two ears.
They
Navigate years.

One from two.

That's one for you.

One step back.

where is your shoe?

I need the honey
And you want the money

But riddle me this
What did you miss?

The sugar
Or the cooker?

The sweets
Or the tweets?

The candy
Or the dandy?

The bun
Or the **fun**?

The sprinkles
Or the mingles?

Do you still want this money?
For that **honey**?

Sniff around my bush
What do you smell?
Rudolph the red nose.
No.
Not red.
Blood.
It's dead.
Watch your head.

What you looking for?
The codes.
The keys.
It might be **under** those **leaves.**
But I'll ask you again...
What you looking for?

Oh... her.
The lady in red.
Ha.
She fled.

You missed her.
Mrs. **Opportunity**
She skedaddled
Gone that way
Yesterday

One-way ticket
Overnight flight
When you were snoring
Memorizing the devil's sins
She visited your kin
Left them a note
Written in red ink
You'll never
See Me again.

But it's night, right?
You still **fly** your kite?
It is night, right?

You fly with no sight
Holding a twisted thread
That fades grey

Melting **in to** the
Mid-night.

But this night
The middle of night.
I can't see right.
Yet you still
Fly your kite.

The twinkle
Of **sapphire** stars

That host the **blue** moon...
Illuminating rooftops.
Where'd it all go?

But tonight
I can't see anything
When I raise my sights
Not even one twinkle
Not even **moonlight**

Your faith
Must be higher than mine.
Hold tight to that thread.
I'll see you in time.

Here is the **light**.
It'll help with sight.
Use your nose.
Avoid the pose.
Sniff around.

You got it.

Nose
With **the** light.
Warmer.
That's right.

There.
A **reflection**.
There.
Shimmering.
You can hear it.

Yeah, use your ear.

No.
Don't fear it.
Just spear it
And clear it.

I'm **try**ing to help.

I know it's messy
I know **it**'s fleshy

I'm just trying to help.

Too much time has passed.
My pains break skin.

My insides **flip**.
I'm speaking crap
And pushing out air.

Oh, where is
The sun?
Who is
Spinning the earth?

Sunlight.
Knock on my door.

Give me my **light** back.
I've been tied in a sack.

    Too long.
      Too long.

I've rolled
Shoulder to shoulder.

    Too much.

      Too many
      Sleepless nights.

It's bed time again

The Devil's
Swift arrow of sin
The pop of my spinal cord
The poison is in.

It's the same
It's the same
All over again.
It's just the same
All over again.

"Like Pulling Scabs"

Have you ever pulled a scab? Have you ever snagged a scab? Tried to rip a scab just to have it drip blood? Yeah... life moments like that.

LIKE PULLING SCABS

Drowning **my scabs**
In kerosene
Alongside
The candle's flame

Scabs bend easier
When they are soaked

How do I know?
I've cried from abuse
Black eye
Open flesh
Cheek bones exposed

Couldn't eat
The belly rumbles
Rumbles quaked
From spine to skull

So, as I unlocked my jaw
Scabs tore
Then the tears rained

Then the scabs **gave way**

That's why I'm soaking
In kerosene
In the candle light

I'll let you know
How this goes.

Each hour
I wipe thoroughly

    Smelly discharge wafts
    From the scabs on my spine.

        ## The pain
        It pierces deep
        Deeper than a lost diamond

Repeated pulses of pain
It's **subdued** when toked
You know
High
Beyond comprehension

    Sprinkling **my** organs with pain pills

      Addiction
      From the roots
      Of one

One scar
One scab
Prescribed by my love

The **remedy**
    These green stars
        These liquids
            These pills

Scabs.

Buzzy-**buzz**

I'm disliking these flies.
Buzzy-buzz
My skin tickling as it dies.

Zip and zoom

Passing **my** ear.
Zip and zoom
They're smelling my fear.

Swipe and swing

Flies picking apart my **ear canal**.
Swipe and swing
I'm trying. Oh Lord, I'm trying.

Jerk **and** twist

My nerves are short circuiting.
Jerk and **twist**

The flies are pulling **death** closer.

Buzzy-buzz
Zipping. Zooming. I'm a maniac.
Buzzy-buzz
Berserk and twerking.

Breathe and choke

Chest cavity exposed. My heart beat **slow**ing.
Buzzy-buzz
Flies planting death in me. Maggots.

BROKEN SCABS

In my cross hairs.
A herd of Oxen.
Stinking.
Fogging the sky
The sun rays are blinking.

It's an Ox.
See? Moron.

As the strife builds
More on
The Ox moves
More on.

Each step I add
More on
Their turf
They just turn
And stomp
And **have fun**
More on.

It's an Ox.
See? Moron.

More on
You stay mad.
More on
They play.

Remember.

It's an Ox.
See? Moron.

Where do we go?

Time keeps moving
I'm moving slow.

Never forget
I am the one
That paid the debt.

I always build
Never alone
With no regret.

There I go
On that road

That scary road
That nobody goes.

BROKEN SCABS

Something subsides **inside** of me
It's brown
It's green
It's ugly
It's mean

Two days ago, I dropped an egg.
It shattered.
Boom, crack. Splattered.

Now, in the midst
Of this second day
I stand.

Did I forget to say?
I left the egg that way.
Molded, green, and grey.

Did I forget to say?
I tore my hair that day.
Uprooting Brown hair.
That hair **dropped** down like a falcon
And tangled with the fallen egg

Did I forget to say I just consumed **it** all?
Two days later.
Hair, mold, green-grey, maggots and **all**.

Did I forget to say?
Something subsides inside of me.
It's brown, it's green, it's ugly, and It's mean.

LIKE PULLING SCABS

A **silly** destiny for a man
Who the next day lost a shoe

Owning one pair only

Not fair
Just...
Isn't fair

Yanking on his hair
Cutting himself
Launching an aerial flare

Vacant **scenes**
Nothing gleams

Now this man's feet
Destined to burn
Destined to leak
Destined to grow scabs
Over scabs
Over scabs
Over bloody
Bloody scabs.

~~Left hand~~ blown away
~~I see~~ things

Dashes with flutters
Shadows within gutters

Ghosts ~~of that destructive day~~
~~I see~~ things

From the corners
Of the walls
Of my eye

Psycho ~~or not~~
~~I see~~ things

Hold on
What's the ~~plot?~~
Wait
I have a thought

The scars of war or not
I just see things

Till my past
Submits to my future
I will not last

My back is scabbed
I know
I know
That's my past

I be insane

See my backside
That's where death resides
Have you heard
Heard what I said

I be insane

Cold granite stone
Heavy on the heart
I can't breathe
A melting furnace
Within the ribs

I be insane

I love the rain
The grey clouds
The thunder
And the lightning pain.

~~Till~~ my past
~~Submits~~ to my future
I will ~~not~~ last

BROKEN SCABS

No shadow.
No silhouette.

It can't reach me.
The real me.
Am I real?
Is it me?

These scabs
Numb me up.
These scabs
Seal me up.

I feel the darkness
Approaching
My doorstep.

Thoughts race sickly
Night by night.
Eyes wide in the dark.
Am I right?

I don't humble
When it's night.
The right of a man
At night.

It's might to night.
From fight to fight.

Vampire's daylight.
I think,
Maybe I'll
Decide my fate
At night.

LIKE PULLING SCABS

I wrote it down
I even carved it
In my skin

It's all scabs now
But they'll soon show
Scar tissue

It'll be useful I tell you
To my eyes
To my memory
To my funeral show

I cut myself
Deep
Deeper than you

Ha-ha
I beat you to it
I cut deeper
Deeper than you ever could

I wrote it down
A message
It teaches
The deeper it cuts
The longer the message remains

I beat you
To my broken heart

Ha-ha
I do more damage to myself
Than YOU

BROKEN SCABS

I cut my eyelids
Took my eyelashes away
I laid myself down
And dreamt away

When I awoke
Scabs had formed
My eyesight **sacrificed**
For the function
Of my flesh

What is **my** scabs teaching?
Me?
Or, am I reaching?

I didn't want to miss anything
Yet now I cannot see.

Scabs scraping my **eyeballs**
Bloody tears
I don't need to see
To know
These are bloody tears
Trickling down me

Now I think I'll miss
Everything

One step forward
Two steps back

The sum of my effort
Mixed with my **fears**

LIKE PULLING SCABS

Pushing my cart.

Scabs dripping pus.

Multiplied

Trail of tears.

Many **fears**

By many years.

My foothold slips
The pus hurls **down**
Beneath my sole
An avalanche came down

My cart of dreams
I push up **the** hill
This **hill** called life
But, I'm losing my feel

Dreams hold on
I've lost my grip
My scabs are infected
Damn it! I tripped.

Will I **sleep** this night?

When my death was shown
A lonely shadow approached.
It screeched into the night.
Finger nails scrape **tight**.
A sound created in spite.

I don't trust the night.
It's where the demons fight.
Oh Father,
Why do I cry at night?

In the thick **sludge of** darkness
My doors are sealed.

The shadow sits still.
Underneath the bed.
A dragon's tongue
At my heel.

The battles are brutal.
Some days I mentally bend.
Sympathetic kin.
A frightful gesture.

A notable **sin.**

At night
my doors are sealed tight.
A man
Watching death approach.

Will I sleep this night?

LIKE PULLING SCABS

My house.
Lights ~~bright.~~
~~Doors~~ shut tight.
Here it is
Dark midnight.

Its sight; stellar.
O Shadow.
Oh silhouette.
My shoulder pet

~~It wants to~~ touch me.
The real me,
What's the decree?

Please. I ask ~~not yet.~~
My house.
Lights bright.
~~Please. I ask~~ not yet.

A demonic silhouette
Feeding off my hate
Feeding off my envy
Feeding off the scabs of my fate.

If this demon gets me
My black scabs
Can feed it
For a century.

It'll turn me.
The revenge in me.
Ninja stars to the throat.
~~It'll~~ kill me.

Flying

I use my bleeding wings
Sleek and scabbed
Shredding wind
Will I crash?

Just a touch
From my past
Propels my sins.

Beyond the cloud
Over the moon
I'm screeching loud

My sick past
What are **the** lessons?

What are the **lessons**?
I desperately ask.

LIKE PULLING SCABS

Blood puddles
From the rain's bows

The lightning **was** worse
A whole town in **a** hearse
A twisted devilish **curse**
Couldn't stop it
Even if they rehearsed

The whole city
The town with no sound
A city **without** a host
Now a city full of ghosts

No need for scabs
When **the flesh** is cold
Cold as glaciers
Served
To the devil's soul

Blood puddles
From the rain's bows

This is
How it goes.

Growing hills.
The grass limbos
Beneath **the wind.**

Now **the rain**
only burns
Against the skin.

No.
Not my sin.
No.
Not **my violin.**

Just the pain
The black scabs
That started
Within **the** wind

Acid rain
The **only** kin
Related
To the wind.

That's trickery.
That is a **sin.**

Head kicking towers.
Thrashing **toward** you.

Twilight nearing
From ocean **piers**.

Slashing apart
The **shape of you**.

                          Message set in scabs.
                          My name **appears**.

Planting fears.
Roots **threading** you.

Do you see it too?
Sucking up **your** tears.

You could never Tip-Toe
Among your **peers**.

"The Nature of the World Stage"

Mother Nature can be cruder than Father Time. Parts of Mother Nature's raw lethal destruction to both physical and mental constructions.

~~Too real~~ to be a scheme
~~Not enough~~ to ~~be~~ a dream
~~My~~ failures are ~~extreme~~
~~My~~ scabs sealing ~~me~~
~~Like~~ a seam

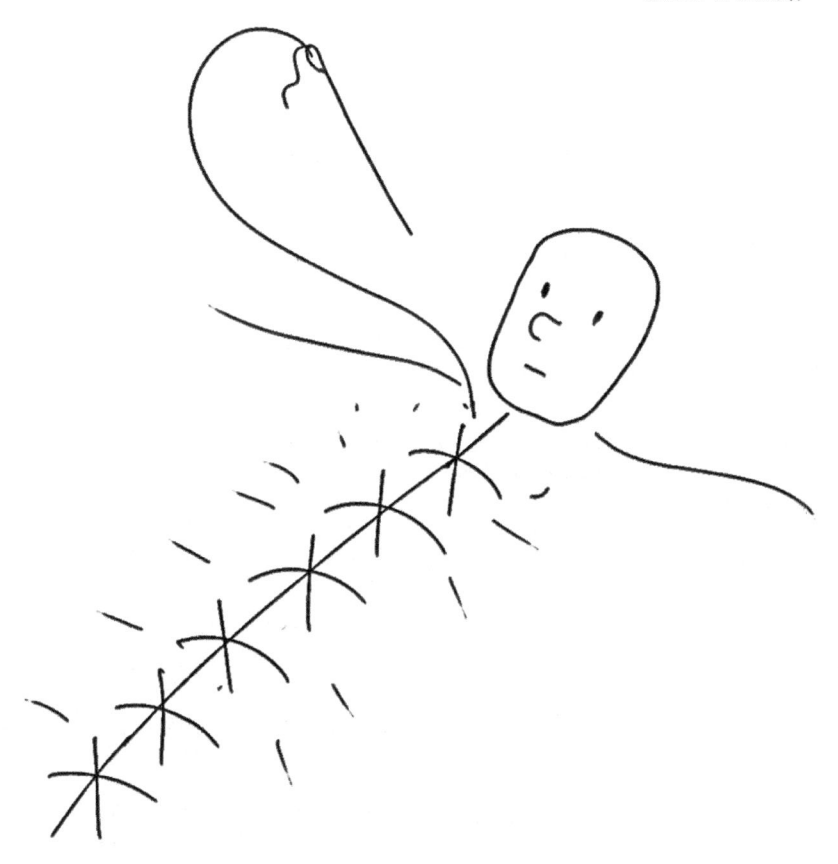

BROKEN SCABS

I panned for gold
Stream to stream.
But I found none.
None **to** be seen.

The few crystals, gems, diamonds, and rings I found
Were bent, cracked, acute, obtuse, and **undefined**.

The luck of a bruised soul
Caged **by** scarred tissue
And bleeding scabs.
Understand **my issue**?

THE NATURE OF THE WORLD STAGE

The soul of my shoes.
~~Man, do I wish~~ you can see
~~The sole of~~ my shoes.

The swamps of Georgia.
The deserts of the Middle East.
The humid nights in Florida.

The refreshing streams
From the Appalachian Mountains.
Cool and fresh for the military teams.

~~The sole of~~ my shoes.
~~The things~~ they've carried
The things they've buried

~~Fear~~ I couldn't ~~budge~~
~~Abuse I had to~~ carry
Heartbreak ~~heaviest~~

The soul of my shoes.
Scar tissue and scabs.
A soul singing the blues.

BROKEN SCABS

As I travel this deep valley of streams
My tote grows heavy.
I'm ~~searching for~~ lost ~~dreams~~.

Nicks and rips.
I lost my maps.
I lost my digging kits.

Soon
There will be no room
For treasures and gifts.

To discern is tough.
I guess I'll drop a trail.
From streams to evergreens
I'll hold this bale.

My ~~pants tight~~
~~Holding~~ rants
Fortified
And sealed.
Dandelions
Red ants.

Will this forest ever yield?

THE NATURE OF THE WORLD STAGE

Welded.

Fortified.
Solid.

There are so many dreams.
It is all up to me.

Welded.
Fortified.
Solid.

My feet are callused
And weary.
Yet **here** I go
Again.

Welded.
Fortified.
Solid.

Dream scene
By dream scene.
By myself.

These feet and **me**.

Welded.
Fortified.
Solid.

~~Soggy limp limb~~
Doctor's know
~~I'm cold~~
~~Done for~~
A fork in the road

THE NATURE OF THE WORLD STAGE

Brittle twig
What happened to you?

You held the fruit
The fruit of **life**
The fruit so sweet
The fruit baked by
Rich rainbow beats.

So brittle **you** look.
I fear to clutch
I fear the snap
I **fear** so much.

I can cover you with chemical.
Would that work for you?
Or do I just chop your soul?
Will that **appeal to** you?

The rain is falling.
Are your warm?
Are you still brittle,
Cold, **scarred, and deformed**?

Where is your bark?
Ouch! I feel your bite.
Piercing. Like a splinter.
Like a brittle twig.
You've lost your right to life.

No starch.

Brittle road.

Sharp.
Made harsh.

Sunlight surface.
Holding still.

No starch.

THE NATURE OF THE WORLD STAGE

~~Stepping through~~ my garden.
~~Rows of brown bear~~ soil.
Plucking the snails.
One. Two. Three.
Time to toil.

~~Muddy shovel cracking~~ the soil
~~Mixing the humus with~~ the dirt
For my roots to chew.

My roots hydrate themselves
Gulping from the dew
While the sun bastes the shoots.

The garden is small.
Tip-toe, tip-toe.
The corn is tall.
What do I sow?

The pods ~~growing large.~~
~~My garden~~ feeling in charge.
Stepping through my garden
~~Rows~~ of brown bear soil.

~~As sudden as~~ headlights
~~As swift as~~ shifting eyes
Grasshoppers ~~and~~ ants
Swarmed ~~my plants~~.

Crunch, chew, swallow...

Now I'm back to ~~only soil.~~
~~They even ate~~ the roots.

- Damn it!

Bright is the flowers
That shine in the day

The moon gives us powers
We need as we lay

THE NATURE OF THE WORLD STAGE

I lost **myself**
This nasty desert
A hero
But no dress shirt

Barbs
No more painful
Than my **failures**
Sealed beneath my scabs

Cactus needles
Clenching my carotid artery shut

Now it is snake scales
Down my throat
Popping venom sacks
Slurping every drop
From **lips** to the desert sand

Waiting for the moon
To sip the bat's blood
The desert night
Cools the finest blood

And after that fine dine wine
I'll sway
On **the spine of the night**
Like a bat
Like a bat... Man

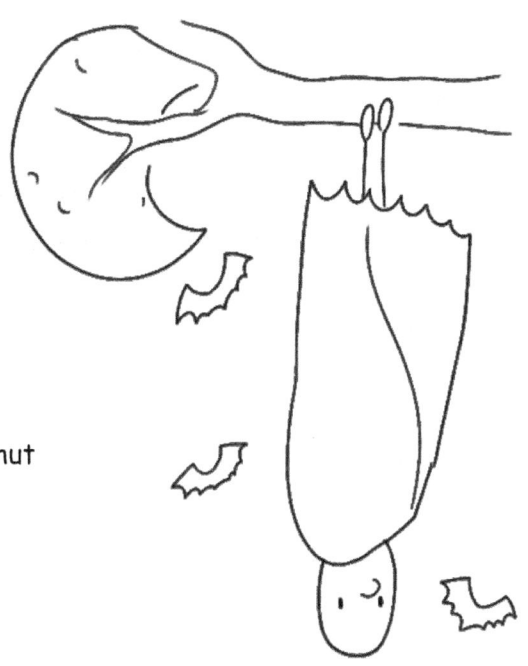

The earth was flat,

But **now** it's round.

                I'll **escape** this way

                       And come back around.

Rain's music audition.
Now just a sound.

The rain was life.

        Now it's **hell**

                All year round.

THE NATURE OF THE WORLD STAGE

Making a world

That **you can**not fix.
Moving along
Picking up sticks.

Build you up.
A world full of sticks.
Breaking you down.
Moving them sticks.

You want some worth?

Pick **up** them sticks.
Build them tall
And avoid conflicts.

I'm making worlds
Using my sticks.

Making a **world**
That you cannot fix.

We are leaves
inside **out**.
Catch what I mean?
Without a doubt.

Every tree added
Opposites appear.
Subtle ways **of life**.
Opposites stay near.

It's called lungs.
It's called fear.
Without the tree
I'm not here.

I need the tree
To put **the** air in me.
You cut down trees
You'll cut down Me

Come find me
In the **trees.**
Can you see me?
I'm in it.
Deep in it.
Like a leaf.

When the heat comes
I grow like leaves and trees.

When **the** wind comes
I swing-dance with the **leaves**.

When hurricanes meet palm trees.
I **line**-dance with the gusty vibes.

When tornadoes twist **the roofs** with twigs.
I salsa-dance with flying figs.

And for the gentle summer wind
I slow-**dance romantic** again.

Cutting up dance floors
On this **earth**.
Follow me.
To a new birth.

I'm the **shade**

The sun keeps **me** paid

Come **with** me

and **you**'ll be saved.

Lightning spears
Electrified
I'm terrified

Between **the** pillars
My spirit
Drifts apart

This **sea**
Sickens
My chemistry.

It's noon
It's soon
Sunny bays
All different ways

This **day** though
Clouds be grey though
At this bay
The sight be grey though

Thoughts are streams.

I just got to find the right one.
From **the** universe they flow.
From the **universe** they go.

Pump **that** gas
Cause here we go.
Pump it fast
Before time catches a cab.
Burning rubber.
Quick son.
My nun-chucks swinging fast.

Dumping **gas**.
Combusting fast.
Juices of our past.
This is our oil.
Our energy.
Can it last?

My red hummer skating
V-8. Two thousand horses.
What **was** that?
Something you can't decode.

Giving me the light.
Turning night bars bright.
Dripping gas from my factory.
Battery after battery.
But, is this friction right? Who knows?

Winters warmer than a **fat belly**.
Oils laboring for us with no complaint.
Goodnight to our toil as we pump this oil.

Extract it fast. The clock ticks.
Tick-tock. Tick-tock.
Vroom. Vroom.
Goodbye... Multiplied by complex tricks.

BROKEN SCABS

The dirt piles.

Rocks different size.
Shapes for all eyes.

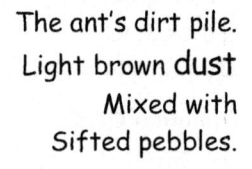

> The ant's dirt pile.
> Light brown **dust**
> Mixed with
> Sifted pebbles.
>
> The gopher's dirt pile.
> Chunky.
> Faded Brown.
> Many **piles abound, all around.**
>
> **The** tractor's dirt pile.
> Bulky jagged rocks.
> Large as my house.
> Dense as Hulk.
>
> **Planet Earth's** dirt pile.
> Dividing valleys.
> Touching the heavens.
> Collecting snow.

Dirt piles beyond sight.
The maker of tools.
Using might.
The ever-giving provider.
Let your **shadows** form
Beneath the yellow sunlight.

Dirt pile power.

Funny bunny

Hip **now** broken.

Hip-**Hopping**
With scars and scabs
Not woken.

No hip. No hop.
No **longer** on top.

No hip. No hop.
Now laying **with** the crop.

Funny bunny
Among the crops.
Fallen and chopped.
You stopped.

Funny bunny
Almost all green.
Sprinkled dirt brown.
Matching the scene.

Funny bunny
It's over.
Nature is mean.
Hip-hop yourself into the ground.
I hope your transfer is clean.

Funny bunny.
Life now over.
Declare your closure
And just get it over.

Sunny days.
Every day.

But this day
clouds be grey.

Longer days
Be black and gray.

And they say
They tend to stay.

THE NATURE OF THE WORLD STAGE

~~Raindrops~~ touch my skin
~~I shake and~~ shiver again
~~Beneath~~ this coat again
Cold ~~and alone~~ again

L.Q. MURPHY

A soaked letter
From the weather
It said for **pleasure**
Find me a feather

I felt pressure
In the lightning weather
Small and lesser
More **like** terror

I stayed clever
I pigeonholed my terror
I found the feather
And I dipped it in pepper
And I **fried** it in **cheddar**

The letter
Never **said** whether
The crow feather
On my hat's leather
Was worse or better
Than one found in weather.

For fun and better
I sent it to my debtor
When I sent the letter
I did not care whether
It went to Heather
Or to Chester
It'll be better
If I know… never.

Nasty rain.

Bringing pain.
You
Have made us
Go insane.

This can't be rain.
I think
It's arrows
Delivered on canes.

Rain from bows.
Shredding **umbrellas**.
Collapsing the crows.

A has been
Taken high.
Rapture.
The clouds
Tell me why.

Nasty **rain**.
Bringing pain.
Why'd you
Make us
Go insane.

Distant clouds thunder
The crack of the boom
Rumbles under.

    Blood puddles.
    Concentric circles.
    Made the **spirits**
    Dive under.

    In the sight of Rainbows
    Dense grey clouds **out west**
    The wind blew
    Then came the rest

Distant clouds **thunder**
The crack of the boom
Rumbles **under**.

    Souls were rolled
    Over red coals.
    Blown down holes
    Where they turned cold.

    Never to be known.
    Drenched and mud sealed.
    Just a soulless hole
    Where they **were killed**.

Distant clouds thunder
The crack of the boom
Rumbles under.

THE NATURE OF THE WORLD STAGE

Everything starts with dirt

The **plant**
The seed
The rock
The land

Everything starts with dirt

The ants
The gem
The ore

The **man**

Everything starts with dirt

The water
The bath
The house
The sand

Everyth**in**g starts with dirt

The rise
The fall
The road
And all

Everything starts with **dirt**

From rain

From snow

Rivers

and streams

Flow

THE NATURE OF THE WORLD STAGE

My breathing release
Be their breathing relief

Their breathing release
Be **my** breathing relief

Yet made from the same
We stay opposite

We cannot forget
We can never be too far.

We need our **star**
With the dirt
The lakes
And the **earth**

The sun ~~and the hills~~
~~The storms and the~~ quakes
~~The wind and the chills~~
The stones and the fields

~~River stones~~
Down the stream
~~They flow.~~

~~This is still~~
~~Why~~ we go.

THE NATURE OF THE WORLD STAGE

Grandma knew I'd write her today
I grabbed the paper and reached for the pen
But then **my** tummy rumbled

I ate and ate
and I ate some more
But then my tummy grumbled

I collided with the carpet
My **eyelids** fell heavy shut
My body crumbled.

I woke **within** a puddle of **vomit**
Stomach acid burning apart my mouth
Coiled shoulder from the tumble.

Grandma dead before I could grab **a** pen.
Discarded opportunity made me feel Dumbo.
Gluttonous sin caused me to fumble.

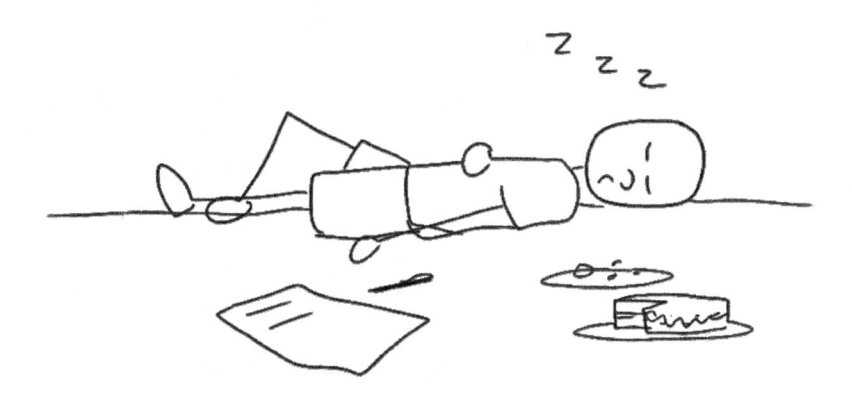

Chasing a bunny
That I could wrap around my wrist.

                Dirt landscape.
                Shovel in hand.
                Hot day.
                Sweaty forehead.
                Huffing in the humid air.
                The bunny is close.
        Digging and **tossing** rocks.
                Deeper and deeper
                Whoa.
                Attempting to run.
                Long drooping ears
              Wrench **the** head

              Where's my **spear**?

                    Quick
                To the heart
                Four-inch blade
                  Pierced
                Through the cage
                  Direct hit
                Heart stopped
                    Rabbit
                    Dead.
                  I got it.
              I got **my** fur.
              Thank you much
                  For the
                Rabbit hair

                              Another life missed.
                                  All for,
                            My brittle **wrist**.

If
If
If **I had**

If I had **two** sunflower seeds

I'd rub them **together**
For the luck
That friction brings

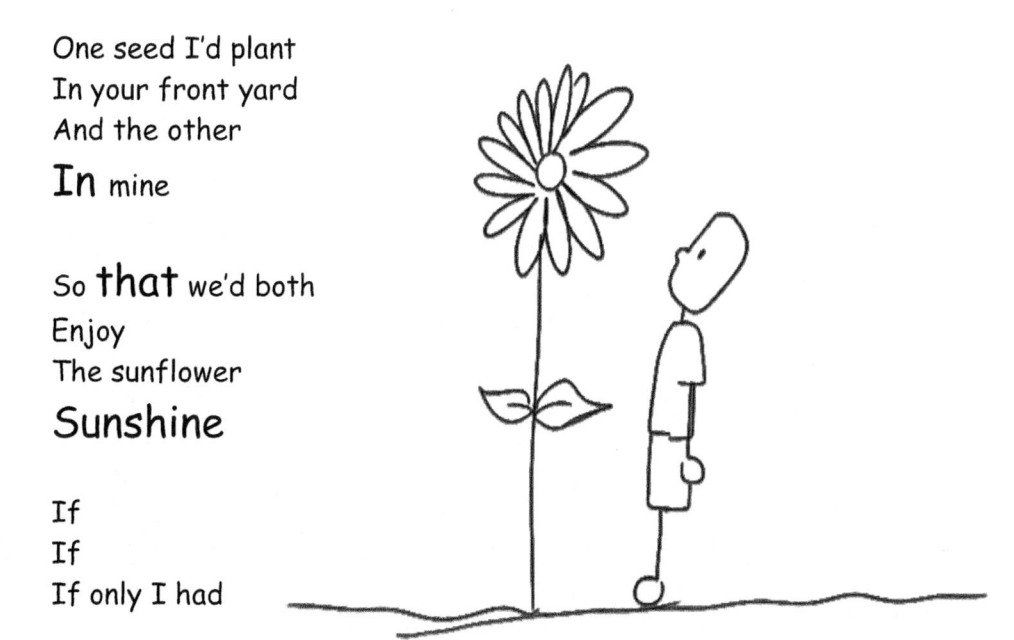

One seed I'd plant
In your front yard
And the other
In mine

So **that** we'd both
Enjoy
The sunflower
Sunshine

If
If
If only I had

BROKEN SCABS

It is orange you say.

It is coming this way, you say.
Then it goes away, you say.

That way, you say?

It makes the flowers open full
It turns the **cold** into warm
It helps the arms **farm**
It makes the rainbows full

I see what you say.
Here it comes this way.

I think I'll stay
As it passes by
This way.

It **is** orange
Like you say.

It happened
Like you say.

Good to see
Another day
And **that** bright orange ball
That passes this **way**.

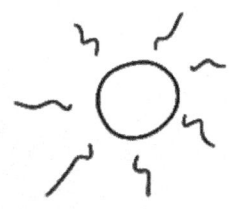

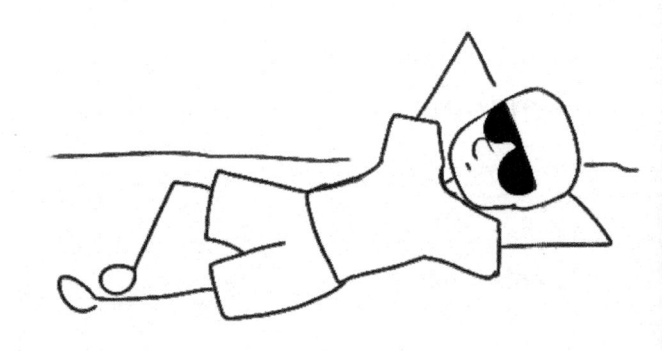

THE NATURE OF THE WORLD STAGE

The whys of life

Why do I cry **inside**?
Why do I cry outside?
Why even cry?
Why even cry why?

Why does the moon not rotate?
It should move like a mill
The moon should have its own ocean
Showing **waves** that **never** sit still

Why do I **sleep** and wake?
The days just take and take.

They take my looks
They take my health
The days just take and take.

Why all of us?
Why is there so many?
Do we have enough?
A penny
For everyone
For each of the many.

Why ask why?
Why do I die?
Why live a life
That begins
And ends
With a cry?

How many **lives** has the ocean consumed?
How many lives has the ocean saved?

Why does the ocean wave?
The ocean **just** waves and waves.

Does the ocean wave to those it saved?
Or does the ocean wave to those who **paid**?

Why does **the** ocean wave?
The **ocean** just waves and **waves.**

No Better Than "Who"

If you have lived longer than twenty years, you might have noticed the way fortunes flip like a morning pancake. One day you are strong, standing high and tall on the mountain called, "Life." The next day you're tumbling down the mountain like a bowling ball looking for the pins. Me, better than you? I guess it depends on the day.

Today is day

Tomorrow is too.

If a man has no foot

Should I have one too?

NO BETTER THAN "WHO"

~~Not the~~ strongest swimmer.

~~A boulder~~
On the lake surface.
~~I sink~~ quick.

I tested my ~~luck~~
~~Swimming~~ streams.
The other day.

To **think**
A shameful scene
In the frog filled stream.

Face **deep**
Was too much
For my clutch.

If I can't
Make it across
What will I do?
What will I do?

Doing time
In the headlight beam

So, I close **my eyes**
And feel for the seam

Nicking knuckles
The **scars** and scabs **extreme**

Yearning for that C.R.E.A.M.
Similar to a dope fiend

NO BETTER THAN "WHO"

I'm back to this red brick home.
The tall glasses.
The delicate plates.
The turkey bones.

Small talk persists as my eyes wander over shoulders.
My eyes are shifting but my mind's eye is fixed.

My legs press me tall at the moment.
Dancing left, with couples to my right.
When the clock tolls
People veer their sight.

Dried bread crust.
Trails of dripping wine.
The masses
Beneath candle lit chandeliers.

Some have had
But nothing sadder to once had.

~~I once had.~~
~~But too bad~~
~~Because~~
~~it was very sad.~~
~~It was very, very, very, very, very SAD.~~

Life drifts across the candle smoke.
A pervasive pungent smell.
Too much of it they say
And you'll choke.

Vroom-vroom
Boom.

Grass grows green.
Leaves produce the scene.

Vroom-vroom
Boom.

Peacocks walk on by.
Pigeons fly by high.

Vroom-vroom
CRACK Boom.

Suddenly
Flies fly away.
Even the ants
Carve a new way.

Vroom-vroom
BIG Boom.

See-You, life.
We couldn't stop.

Cars backfire

~~WHAT'S NEXT?~~
When will we stop?

I hide from fright
Within my head.
Shaking hard
Within my bed.

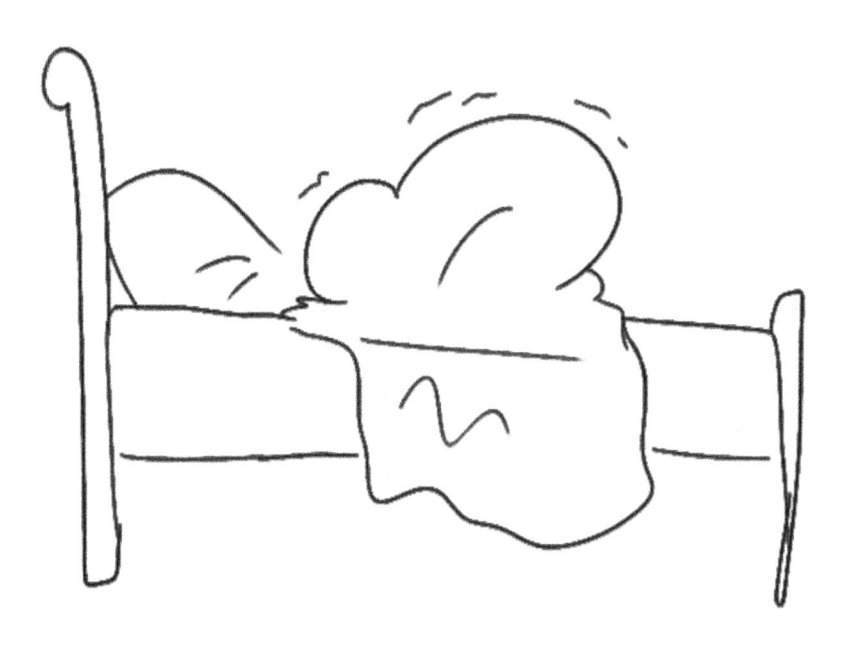

Running about the flurry hill
The feet of many mice

Running **about the** flurry hill
The blood of manly fights

Running about the flurry **hill**
The lives of men and mice.

NO BETTER THAN "WHO"

Within the same day
I ask myself
Will **chickens** fly
Up within
The vast blue sky?

    Maybe chickens
    Will eat us all.

Gang up
Cut our throats
Compress the blood free
Free flowing
Down the concrete street

Flip flop **us**
In corn meal
Garlic. Salt. Pepper.
And who can forget
The onion peels.

    Just a thought.
    A moment.
    Captured
    While I eat.

Pass the ketchup please.
This fried chicken
Taste even better
With mac n cheese.

L.Q. MURPHY

Read this
I say

I be crazy
I not lazy

I eat blue flames
I gnaw on your brains

I Indian-burn you
I **deep** sea drown you

I plant grenades **in your chest**
I give you both red and blue pill when you rest

I not like the rest
I stop thunder with my chest

I shatter lightning bolts
I soak in the lightning's volts

Read this
I say

A treasured lesson
I say

It's wisdom
I say

Jingle. Keys jingle.
Let's start.

Swift pass
The red light.
That's me.
Where's the fork?
Road rage.
Oh wait,
I **see it.**
Crash.
Boom!
Grab the broom.

Jingle. Keys jingle.
Let's start.

My keys dangle.
The door to hell
Right in front of me.
Insert key.
Insert me.
Clomp. Clomp.
Stomp by stomp.
Flicking flames.
Taking names.

Yeah, that's **me.**
Jingle. Keys jingle.

My tail.

Smacking your face.
You follow me.
You must **can't**
Keep your pace.

No brakes
When I make my **move**.

Breached a door.
Goliath.
His door.
Next.
Your door.

Dead bolt.
Claymore.
Laser sights.
Figure-four.
They won't help
Anymore.

Sweat trickles
Behind your ear.
It pours
And it pours.

My **tail.**
That's where you'll be.
Follow me.
You must can't see.

There are two.

One.
Two.

Two roads.

One.
Two.

One for me.
One for you.

One avoided.
One trampled.

One new.
One sampled.

There's a division
Implied
Let's just pray
You get it right

There are two.

One for me.

One for **you**.

The tree branches
I be

My hair
The leaves

My skin.
The bark.

This land.
My mark.

The Redwood tree
My posture be

The tree branches
I be

My hair
The leaves

~~Avoiding~~
~~Matches~~
Nothing matches
Me

NO BETTER THAN "WHO"

Pitter-patter
Across the
numbers
On the clock.

Time is
As it seems

What do I mean?

Does it matter?

Time still rows by.
~~Back muscles strong~~
But I
~~never~~
Look back.

The story
Of time
On the climb
~~To glory~~

~~What~~ is it you ~~ask~~?

A light
A spark
A fire
A flame

I need the light too.

~~I'm like you too.~~

I need sight
I need the first step
I need to make way for new life
I need to carry that ability with me

It's interesting
What you listed.

Is this what you need?

Is this ~~what~~ you ~~ask~~?

"Abstract Exposer"

This section can only be communicated using fascinatingly incomprehensible poetic stories. Although challenging to comprehend the message at first, the reader will have acquired the most elusive prize of life at the end... communication with the deepest part of the soul.

Do I owe you my soul?
Do I owe you a toll?
Can I give you a hug?
~~Please,~~ understand my soul.

ABSTRACT EXPOSER

More questions ~~than me~~?
I think not.
I think not.

More guesses ~~than me~~?
I think not.
I think not.

More wonder ~~than me~~?
I think not.
I think not.

More confusion ~~than me~~?
I think not.
I think not.

More problems ~~than me~~?
I think not.
I think not.

The wind that pushes
Is the wind that pulls.
The heart I have
For **lovers and fools**.

The moment now
Is all I've known.
The forever day
Is all that's **known.**

The heart I have
That pushes and pulls
Is the same both ways
For lovers and fools.

My soul knows better.

My **soul** knows more.

Watch it happen.

The **swirls** and more.

Watching my pearls
Around these swine.

ABSTRACT EXPOSER

Was **I** told

Blue and red
Make the purple hues?

I only see
Red roses
And blue roses.

~~Where~~ are those roses with the purple hues?

I was told
Blue and red
Make the purple hues.

I only see
Red blood
and tears from the blues.

~~Where~~ are those sweet purple hues?

I was told
Blue and red
Make the purple hues.
So, here is what I'll do.

My blood is red.
This water is blue.

I flip myself

Just for you.
Now my skin
A purple hue.

Greener leaves taste better.

BROKEN SCABS

I told my little garden friends.

That is good. The grasshopper declared.
The grasshopper **told** the snail.

That is good. The snail declared.
The snail told the caterpillar.

That is good. The **cat**erpillar declared.
The caterpillar told the rabbit.
The rabbit just stared back.

The caterpillar spoke again
Asking if the rabbit understood.

Now, what happened next
Freaked the garden crew **to** their spinal bones.
It even flipped the nerve signals of myself.

A grindy, raspy voice; slow in tempo said,
"I **eat** the flesh and bones of the black bats."

Well, the rabbit spoke.
It turned and limped off.
Dripping a green wax from its ears.

We gathered close together.
Watching the ghastly **blood** consuming creature leave.

"I think I'll stick with green leaves,"
I told my little garden friends.

They agreed green was better

ABSTRACT EXPOSER

Ax in my right hand
Swaying past my thigh

Repeating inside
You die
You die

Another day
~~Don't~~ cry
~~Don't~~ cry

Stay afar
~~Or you'll~~ die
~~Or you'll~~ die

Generations
Been scarred
Been scarred

My destiny
It's tarred
It's tarred

Ax in my right hand
Swaying past ~~my thigh~~

Repeating inside
~~You~~ die
You ~~die~~

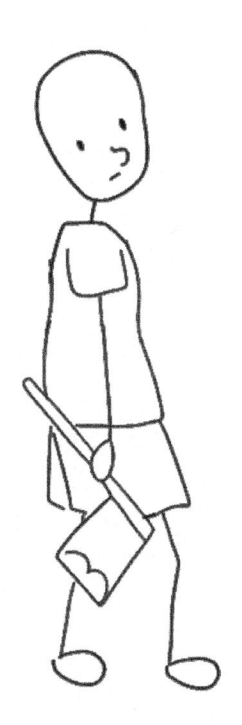

Many dreams ~~sewn~~
~~The seams~~ are strong.

~~None~~ torn.
~~Flames~~ of fear
Where the dreams are born.

Many dreams sewn.
These seem strong.

ABSTRACT EXPOSER

Born and born
and re-born again.
Three lives.
Each one together.
Airtight as a **fist**.

Using what **I've** learned
It's a risk.
A **tilted** sight.
In the mist.

But it's like... list after list.
One for **my heart**
And one
For those that depart.

To the heavens.
To the earth.
To the flesh I have.

Three lives.
I
Brother
Mother

The rebirth of masks
Dripping salty fluid.
The face of poker players.
Airtight as a fist.

Too **old**.
I don't know.

Heart beat low.
Tow to tow.
Hitching now.
Too old.

Here I go.
There I go.
Dreaming.
Deceiving.

Seeming.
Teaming.
Screaming.
Believing.

Gut churning.
Over hills.
Cheers up
Then down
With a spill.

Can it be?
It's over.
Too dizzy
To see over.

To **be**
Or not to be?
A legend?
Or a flea?

ABSTRACT EXPOSER

I think I'll die at night

It's my thought.
Is it right?

I don't sleep.
This can't be right.

I think I'll die at night.
Will that scene
Make it right?

We will
One day see
One moonlit
Blue-grey night.

An inviting site
Witnessed at night.

I think I'll die at night
In the bright moonlight.

I ~~don't~~ want to sleep.
~~Fear sits~~ atop my bed frame.

My palms ~~dripping sweat.~~
~~Heartbeat~~ playing hopscotch in my chest.

Alone in a dream
Near the valley's stream.

Sipping the H2O.
~~It's tainted~~ with fish ~~scales.~~

I don't want to sleep.
I know fear sits atop as I weep.

~~Performing its~~ plots.
~~Twisting my veins~~ in knots.

So never mind the blood clots.
And never mind the thorny rocks.

There's a visual within my scream
Roller coaster loops within my dream.

But again,
I ~~don't~~ want ~~to sleep~~.
Fear ~~sits atop my bed frame.~~

~~I don't want~~ to sleep.

My eyesight ~~vacates~~.
~~Lids~~ tight.

I can see
My heartbeat.
Fall ~~face first~~.

What's this?
GOD?

Ignorance?
It's bliss.

~~It is we?~~
GOD and I.
~~Judgement~~
In the sky.

My soul.
~~The token.~~
The fee.
~~It's me.~~

Eyes wide as valleys
I'm issued my fate
~~Is~~ the great gift grace~~?~~
Or is it ~~just too late~~?

The sharp **everlasting** pain.

Love me.
Await me.
Even if there is **rain**.

The heavens
Why so high?

This ground
It **is** fashioned
With
The devil's caption.

Strategic blow.
It's **draining my** eyes.

The sharp everlasting pain.

You can **sense** it
Every time I sigh.

ABSTRACT EXPOSER

Speed limit.
Long forgotten.

My speedometer
It's gone rotten

Blinker on.
Merging into the wall.
I don't back down.
Who will fall?

Speed limit.
Long forgotten.

My speedometer
It's gone rotten.

Brake line cut.
I did that.
Egg on the wall.
Desires gone splat.

Speed limit.
Long forgotten.

My **speed**ometer
It's gone rotten

Touch down.
Not me.

Home **I** run.
Off the runway.
The dragon's cave.

That's what I **crave**.

Piranha rivers.
Diving headfirst.
Brain flesh.
Competing zombies.
The toll these days.

Before Goliath.
Destination hell.
Churning the wheels.

Freight train **density**.
The Mad-Man's trail.

Touch down.
Not me.
Home I run.
Off the runway.
Hell's archway.

That's what I crave.

ABSTRACT EXPOSER

Intense **cas**es
Of insight

Bleak understandings
Having their way

Re-presenting **themselves**
This way
Today

Converting

To **in**stant
Blobs of memory

Sensual
Is the imagery

My insight
Re-presenting
Pathways

The pulse
Of a sinner

One
And two.

What would **you** do?

One
Sunshine.

Time
Sublime.

From sleep
I wake.

Age
And time.

Life's
Next crime.

One
Sunshine
For this earth

I take
And bake

Basics
That work.

Rub **the fur**ry bunny
on my big O tummy

Feel the warm **sunny**
and eat some **honey**

I will get there

There...

~~To the top~~

With the life-giving crop

The crop of eternity
The land that's scented
Where freedom is gifted
With perjury that's tilted

On the fast side

Of the highway entrance

Going for a ride

Just an **apprentice!**

In your face
Do you follow?
To the top
I fly
Like a swallow

The **end?**

The end.

Oh crap!

Yup,

This is the end...

The END.

Yes
The ending
Is always hard

But
I promise
You'll see me
Again

I
Sign off
Here

I promise
This is not
My END!

Author

Born, in 1983, to an African American family (descendent from slavery) in Salinas, California, Lawrence Murphy Jr. joined the United States Army at age eighteen to become a United States Army Airborne Ranger. During his service, he deployed four times to combat zones: two times in support of Operation Enduring Freedom (the war in Afghanistan, 2001) and two times in support of Operation Iraqi Freedom (the war in Iraq, 2003). After his military service, Lawrence Murphy Jr. pursued studies of business finance at Fresno State University, achieving distinction; earning the graduating status of cum laude. During college, he met his wife. They have two children. Lawrence enjoys reading, writing, studying martial arts, watching movies, and enjoys warm spring afternoons with family and friends.

L.Q. Murphy,
Author of *Broken Scabs*
Instagram: @lq.murphy

written by, L.Q. Murphy

"Gift Yourself Insightful, Therapeutic Poetry"

The I in my Eye
L.Q. Murphy

Dark poetry with art ready to help you rethink the world. Intense emotions from the poetry make the mind rethink. Poetry and art help readers learn more about human nature. This book is a mixture of poetic themes. **eBook, paperback, and hardcover**

- ***Shimmering Parts of Her***
  L.Q. Murphy

This particular book of this ongoing poetry book series, called SCABS, adds a piece of artwork that expresses the deep appreciation of the female. The book discusses the intricate and immersed wisdom observed by the male counterpart. The greatest life lessons many men will learn and employ in daily life will have derived from the supervision and authority of the females in that male's life. Then a male's education continues, perpetually, as he learns from the purposeful and chance meetings with his female counterparts that he will meet and know. As a result, his quality of life and the quality of society will bend toward happiness and fulfillment. **eBook, paperback, and hardcover**

Afterword

"Thank YOU"

"I write to help others gain insight into the mysteries of life including the emotions of love, hate, courage, fear, joy, despair, achievement, and disappointment."

"My poetic stories can be abstract yet very entertaining."

"I am grateful. That is all that I am. I think life waits, basically bored, just waiting for all of us to experience it. Congratulations! You just now did that. And... the universe thanks YOU for that. I, definitely, thank YOU for allowing me to serve YOU."

- **L.Q. Murphy** *(father, husband, U.S. Army veteran, author)*

Printed in Great Britain
by Amazon